PLOTINUS BLUSHED

PLOTINUS BLUSHED

Jim Chapson

ARLEN HOUSE

Plotinus Blushed

is published in 2013 by
ARLEN HOUSE
42 Grange Abbey Road
Baldoyle
Dublin 13
Ireland
Phone/Fax: 353 86 8207617
Email: arlenhouse@gmail.com

Distributed internationally by
SYRACUSE UNIVERSITY PRESS
621 Skytop Road, Suite 110
Syracuse, NY 13244–5290
Phone: 315–443–5534/Fax: 315–443–5545
Email: supress@syr.edu

ISBN 978–1–85132–049–3
limited edition hardback

Typesetting by Arlen House
Printing by Brunswick Press

Contents

this book is for
Aodh
always
&
E.A., J.S., P.V.

THE BOOK

It's dark now, you've been trudging
through snow for hours; what began
as a pleasant walk has become a chore.
At last a lighted window shows an inn.
It is warm inside, with the comforting
smells of beer and tobacco.

A stranger, you are greeted politely,
with suspicion. You order a beer, and the men
who turned to observe you entering
now turn away, but are listening carefully.

The Castle, invisible on the hill above,
owns the village; you are not allowed
to stay the night without permission,
which finally comes by phone.

From this point on, your attempts
to discover whether the Castle
has any work for you end in frustration.

You want desperately to unravel
the ambiguities that have overtaken you,
but the author of this story died long ago,
leaving it unfinished, and anyone
opening the book and turning its pages,
will sympathize, but be unable to help you.

Maybe it would have been better
if the story had never been written,
but it's too late: the book is on the shelf;
the Castle looms over the village.

THE SUN IS THE SIZE OF A HUMAN FOOT

– Heraclitus, fr. 3

Maybe things really are
what they appear to be:

the sun is the size of a human foot;
it is warm and good;
therefore, its creator loves us.

A stranger approaches with hands open
in friendship.
Why should we doubt this?

The stars in fact
are pin pricks in the firmament
beyond which lies
the inconceivable realm of light.

Of course there is no reason to believe
the fragment means what it appears to mean.
Heraclitus may have meant
nothing is what it seems to be:

the sun is monstrously large;
the open hands a deception.

Who can know?
It would seem that skepticism is warranted,

but this might be a preference
not shared by Heraclitus

who said, *The sun is new each day* (fr. 6).

Now There Was a Gate

Those who'd come this way before,
told of hearing from beyond the wall
a murmuring of liquid voices,
intriguing and attractive;
the wall itself appeared impenetrable,
though the path which lead to it
continued on the other side.

But now there was a gate,
an opening, narrow,
and without the daunting gatekeeper
of the rabbi's parable,
and so accessible, it seemed,
even to us.

Surveying the entrance,
we found it wet with blood
which gave us pause
balancing the attraction from beyond.

We considered offering a sacrifice
appropriate to the occasion,
then passing through,
but the consensus was to follow the wall
in search of a passage more welcoming,

which we have been doing now
for years to no avail,
while subsequent expeditions to the gate
have reported the blood on the stones
still wet.

Mullah Omar contemplated
the Buddhas of Bamiyan, two statues
carved in a sandstone cliff,
their solid immensity misleading
worshippers for a thousand years.

The monk is one who turns away
from material shapes, thought Mullah Omar;
impermanent and unstable
are all conditioned things.
If one has the apprehension of an object,
then the whole net of discursive ideas
comes about, but where there is nothing,
nothing is grasped. One who is convinced
of the emptiness of everything
has no likes or dislikes; he knows
whatever he might like is just empty.

The ultimate reality is emptiness.

He opened the Heart Sutra:
Form does not differ from emptiness;
emptiness does not differ from form.
Form itself is emptiness; emptiness form.

Mullah Omar meditated deeply
upon these precepts.

A Talk with the Heart

Who can lay hold on the heart and give it fixity,
so that for some little moment it may be stable,
and for a fraction of time may grasp the splendour
of a constant eternity?
— Augustine, *Confessions*

He was lying in bed waiting for sleep
to bring its possibilities
when his heart banged out a number
of irregular rhythms, demanding attention
like a drummer taking his solo.

Time for a talk with the heart, he thought.
He thanked it for being the steady one
in the relationship, apologized
for being so dependent, let it know
its long service was not unappreciated.

His heart replied it wasn't asking
for recognition, that if he thought its toil
was on his behalf, he was mistaken;
it had its own agenda. The heart breaks,
heart throbs, heart felt desires, were all his doing.
In its heart of hearts it desired stillness.

He said to his heart, 'I understand',
but he didn't. He said, 'I'm sorry',
but he wasn't. He said, 'from now on …',
but didn't know what came after that.

PROPHETS

*Now after [the magi] had left, an angel of the Lord appeared to Joseph
in a dream and said, 'Get up, take the child and his mother, and flee to
Egypt' … When Herod died, an angel of the Lord suddenly appeared
in a dream to Joseph in Egypt and said, 'Get up, take the child and his
mother, and go to the land of Israel …'*

– Matt 2.13, 19–20

Egypt! Israel! What the fuck!
Joseph just wanted to settle down
and raise the bastard kid someplace
where nobody would stone his wife –
the boy looked nothing like him.

*There he made his home in a town called Nazareth,
so that what had been spoken through the prophets
might be fulfilled …* (Matt 2.23)

Fulfilling the words of the prophets
maybe was not such a good idea;
prophets usually had it in
for just about everyone – did they ever say,
'you're going to get laid by a real beauty',
or, 'you'll win the lottery'?
No, more like, *Devastation and destruction,
famine and sword – who will comfort you?* (Is 51.19)

But fulfilling a prophecy wasn't a choice,
or maybe it was but the prophet knew
what choice you'd make. Our ruling passions
are easy enough to read,
and if yours isn't football, power, or poontang,
you're probably going to get screwed.
But this kid was destined for big things – the messiah.
That was cool. Or maybe not. It depends.

Anyhow, it goes to show you can't hide out
even in a hick town like Nazareth –
those prophets and angels will track you down.
And if the fulfillment is never what you hoped for,
it's a fulfillment all the same.

THE STORY OF THE BRICK

He remembered the story of the brick:
There was once a brick that grew tired
of its place, was about to give in,
collapse, let the others hold things up,
when it had a vision, or at least
a voice: 'it's true', said the voice,
'you're just a brick like the others, but in fact,
if you give in the whole wall comes down'.

The story was meant to lift him
from despondency – your life, it said,
has significance beyond your knowing;
or did it mean, you have the power
to bring ruin – like Samson pulling the temple
down to crush himself and the Philistines?

But what was the wall? A protective barrier,
or an obstacle?

That's the problem with parables:
to interpret them rightly, you must first
know their meaning: they confirm in their knowledge
those who know, and for the others provide
a puzzle, like a bone thrown to a dog
to distract it from interfering,
while thieves go about their business.

Plotinus Blushed

*One day Origen came to the conference room; Plotinus blushed deeply
and was on the point of bringing his lecture to an end; when Origen
begged him to continue, he said, 'The zest dies down when the speaker
feels that his hearers have nothing to learn from him'.*
            – Porphyry, *On the Life of Plotinus*

You know the feeling – you're delivering
your most profound half-truths
to a new victim when you see
an old friend listening, smirking,
and you stammer, caught out.

Of course if you happen to be Plotinus
this doesn't happen very often; in fact,
it never happens at all – your students
have come to absorb from the master
the neoplatonic mysteries.

They reverence you; everyone does,
except those ignorant and gullible Christians
conned by their priests – except for Origen
who knows all you know, yet believes
the absurd dogma of the Christians.

He knows, yet he believes; it's unnerving.
If he believes although he knows,
he doesn't know; if he believes because
he knows, you're left standing in front
of the conference room with nothing to say.

In Heaven the Dead

In heaven the dead write poems
for the dead; they are not celebrations
of the departed life,
to which they refer as 'the dark time',
amazed how it held them once.

The poems of the dead are gratuitous:
a light rain on a sunny day.

They need no metaphors: nothing
needs explaining in terms of something else
where everything is evidently itself.

The poems of the dead require
no analysis: they are not products
of imagination, that dim lantern mortals use
to illuminate obscurity.

The poems of the dead are never revised,
they simply occur like sunlight through leaves.

The dead write poems for the dead
in greeting, never farewell.

The dead write no poems for the living.
Let them, they say, sing their own songs;
let them weep tunefully for us,
as if death were something to lament.

THE OLD

Remember not the events of the past,
the things of long ago consider not;
see, I am doing something new!
Now it springs forth, do you not perceive it?

– Isaiah 43.18–19

They meet to reminisce.
No one understands them anymore.
They bore the young with litanies of pain,

their failing bodies now
their sole attachment to a world
that's had enough of them.

Wars and lies and politics go on,
and the young are worried over many things;

the old know anyone can love,
and no one cares about your troubles.

They sit in malls and coffee shops,
discuss the newest medications
and the latest deaths,

content,
in spite of having left so much undone.

So you, you strap my splendid armor on your back,
you lead our battle-hungry Myrmidons into action.
                                        – The Iliad 17.73–74

While he wore Achilles' armor,
no one could touch him, warriors fled
in fear. Achilles could hang back
safe at his ships, indulging his bitterness,
while Patroclus pushed the Trojans back
to the walls of Troy, returning safely
so Achilles could step in to battle
at the city's gates, killing Hector,
winning honour.

But there couldn't be two Achilles,
one sulking at his ships, one on the battlefield
(Patroclus disguised as Achilles) charging
his enemies, dodging arrows and spears.

Achilles wanted too much and the gods
wouldn't have it. Apollo stepped in,
tore from Patroclus
Achilles magnificent armor, wrenched
the spear from his hands, so the coward
Euphorbus could hurl a lance
in his back and run, leaving Patroclus
naked, helpless, wounded
in front of the powerful Hector
who rammed a spear through his guts.

Nothing remained for Achilles
but to take his place on the battlefield,
kill Hector and soon himself be killed.
The gods knew it. Achilles knew it.

Even his horses knew it,
and were happy to remind him of it,
still grieving as they were over the death
of Patroclus whom everyone loved.

Dreaming & Waking

Peter said to him in reply, 'Lord, if it is you,
command me to come to you on the water'.
He said, 'Come'. Peter got out of the boat
and began to walk on the water toward Jesus.

– Matt 14.28–29

We all know what happens next,
even those who've never heard the story:
Peter sinks.

Sometimes in dreams the air has a certain
substantial feel; you can push yourself
up in it, remembering you always
knew you could fly, and then you wake up
earthbound.

Was Peter dreaming the dream of faith
when the storm hit and woke him up
and he began sinking? If he'd kept dreaming
could he have walked all the way to Jesus on the water?

It had been a long day and Peter was sleepy.
When he saw Jesus walking toward him
he woke up, stepped out onto the solid water,
fell asleep, and started sinking.

In the dream of flying you knew
you could always fly, but when Peter
woke up and stepped out of the boat
he knew he'd never done this before.

When the wind shook him, he took his gaze
off the beloved face, fell asleep, dreamed
he was sinking; in the dream Jesus
came to lift him. Peter woke up.

'You were doing fine', said Jesus;
'when you think about it, water is pretty solid –
you always knew you could walk on it'.

Curiosity

The mars-lander Curiosity has landed
in a landscape, scientists say,
remarkably like one of earth's deserts.

Getting there required
the perfect functioning
of an elaborate mechanism:
the descent with the heat-shield
jettisoned at the right moment,
the giant parachute deployed
then released, the retro-rockets firing,
the winching down by cables
from a sky-crane
which then takes off – a sequence
so bizarre only a child
could have imagined it, only
obsessive engineers made it work.

And so our Curiosity is now on Mars,
our careful attention, our
desire to know, our
inquisitiveness
which leads us always elsewhere.

We might discover water,
or evidence that water once was there
which might mean life
existed once and may have left
some traces still.

However, there are rumors life
existed once on earth
and left some traces here;
we might discover whether

it could be here still,
but we prefer to keep
our Curiosity on Mars,
where it will rove for years –
a useless if remarkably ingenious
piece of human workmanship;
in fact, a curiosity.

Q. Why do journalists refer to the Higgs boson as the 'God particle'?
A. Because they are atheists.

Q. Who is 'Biggs'?
A. Peter Biggs is a theoretical physicist who did important work in the field in the 1960s.

Q. What is a 'boson'?
A. 'Bosun' is a common abbreviation of 'boat swain', a ship's warrant officer. 'Boson' is a typo for 'bison', a large gregarious quadruped with a shaggy mane and short black horns which once roamed in herds over much of the temperate zone of North America. While it is difficult to imagine scientists mistaking a large shaggy quadruped for a subatomic particle, it is equally hard to see how they could confuse a bison with a ship's warrant officer. However, we must remember that in exploring the world of particle physics many of our most cherished assumptions about reality are likely to be overturned.

Q. Why has it taken so long to find it?
A. Scientists erred in using the Large Hadron Collider to search for something infinitesimally small. Had they employed a Small Hadron Collider, they would likely have found it much sooner. It is easier to find a needle in a sewing basket than in a haystack; indeed, while many needles have been found in sewing baskets, scientists have yet to find one in a haystack.

Who Could Blame Them

They intended to reshape the world –
who could blame them?
To make it amenable to the success of trade,
bringing prosperity, democracy, and freedom
to those who longed for them, or would do so
once they had tasted their possibilities.

Tyrants, of course, had first to be removed
along with their bands of blind adherents,
surgically: pain and discomfort passing quickly,
the social body restored, stronger than before,
objecting skeptics silenced by the operation's success,
of which there could be no doubt.

As it turned out, the liberation did not proceed
entirely as planned: the beneficiaries
acting contrary to self-interest failed to grasp
the opportunities offered them
now lying unrealized amid the ruins and butchery.

And then there were those
who approached the threshold
but at the last moment drew back,
unwilling to cross over.

We cajoled them, reached out,
took their hands in ours,
gently, to persuade them,
but they were not ready,

to use force was forbidden,
and we were not allowed
to encourage them by
stepping over to the other side.

They'd turn away, hesitate,
come back; we did all we could
to appear welcoming.

There must have been
something disturbing
they saw in us which
we could not ourselves see:

perhaps it was the radiance
obliterating our faces.

Once John Ashbery dreamt he was John Ashbery, John Ashbery fluttering around, happy with himself, doing as he pleased. He didn't know he was John Ashbery. Suddenly he woke up and there he was, solid, unmistakable John Ashbery. But he didn't know if he was John Ashbery who had dreamt he was John Ashbery, or John Ashbery dreaming he was John Ashbery. Between John Ashbery and John Ashbery there must be some distinction!

THE REAL THING

Because previous attempts to reintroduce captive pandas
into the wild have been largely unsuccessful,
researchers have developed the novel technique
of dressing as the animals to acclimate them to the wild.

– Time.com

I could've sworn they were pandas –
fuzzy, with our distinctive markings.
They brought me bamboo shoots,
showed me the way to the clear stream.

It was only when they left me
deep in the forest that I discovered
the deception. Real pandas smell funky,
are not always so nice, and think like pandas.

It's tough in the forest, competing
with other pandas for finite resources.
The fake pandas helped each other out.
We don't cooperate, and keep pretty much
to ourselves except for mating every year
or two. I haven't tried it yet but hope to
soon, and not with some sick furry
in a panda suit.

Anyway,
with our low birth rate and shrinking habitat,
we'll soon die out, to be replaced
by panda coffee mugs, key chains,
a few tame pandas kept in a nature park.
Nobody wants the real thing:
alien wild pandas, unpredictable, with teeth.

The Official Histories

… and he was with the wild beasts
and the angels ministered to him.

> – Mk 1.13

They hadn't been told they were angels.
If they had, they wouldn't have submitted
their applications to the demiurge
offering positions as commanders
of new worlds spinning off
as quickly as they could be imagined.

In charge of one of these, they'd hold
countless souls cowering, eager to please,
but as angels they were *persona non grata;*
they belonged to the other side,

and so were disappointed to find themselves
in a wretched desert of poisonous reptiles,
rocks, and thirst, keeping hyenas away
from a scrawny Jew with an identity crisis
while he was being tempted by 'the adversary'
who'd come out of nowhere, full of reasoning,
a member of the debate team, a sophist, a lawyer.

The job was nothing to be proud of; they didn't
even put it in their résumés, so their names
were never recorded in the official histories:
Joe, Steve, Eddie.

Last week I was walking along the shore of lake
Michigan when I saw an angel coming over the water
carrying a torch in one hand and a bucket in the other.
Do you think that you can put out the fires of Hell
with that bucket of water, I asked him, burn down the
mansions of Heaven with that torch?

O, it's a never-ending task, he said, never ending. It's
hard work, but I have to keep at it, because if I can put
out the fires of Hell then people won't be afraid, and if
I can burn down the Mansions of Heaven people
won't need anything. And when no one is afraid or
needy, they'll be able to love each other as they
should.

That's it.

CLOUD

— Lk 9.34

The cloud took everything away.

They couldn't see each other,
and were afraid, but when it lifted

the voice was gone and the dazzling angels;
the transfigured Master was himself again.

What good was all this show if afterwards
everything was as it was before?

Like a magician's trick – after being sawed in half
the lady emerges whole.

They all went down the mountain.

Maybe it had just been lightning –
or some kind of cloud inversion.

If God had shown Himself and spoken,
wouldn't everything be different?

Nothing had changed, but everything
that had engaged them once seemed pointless now.

Q. Why have scientists been so eager to find this particle?

A. Proof of this particle's existence confirms the Standard Model, the foundation of physics for the last fifty years, as an experimentally verifiable reality, and not merely a delusion like all previous models.

Natural

That it is natural for people
to help one another, advancing
the common good, willingly
forsaking personal gain
so that the weaker, the less
competent, those more in need
might have adequate provision,

is viewed cynically by those
to whom this doctrine is an excuse
by which the lazy benefit
from the hard work of the virtuous,
by which they mean themselves,

and so it is only natural
they form a party to promote
their interests, because the weak,
the incompetent, and the needy,
cannot be counted on to advance
the agenda of the strong,
for whom were made
all the good things of the world.

among those who worship them
is noticed, appreciated; and the audience,
departing, turns its thoughts to dinner,
wine, and sex, as the Gods of Reason flicker,
disappear.

It hadn't been a bad trip on the whole.
Things had gone, by and large, pretty well;
periods of boredom came and went,
the other passengers were diverting,
but as we neared Byzantium
we felt uneasy, to tell the truth;
the journey had been so long we'd forgotten
our destination, even that there was one,
had settled in to a daily round of meals,
strolling the deck, nightly movies,
drinks with friends; we didn't really
want it to end. Some were locking
themselves in their cabins, others were ill;
we were all a bit queasy entering the harbor,
seeing for the first time the people of Byzantium
in their bright silks, odd headgear. Were these
the friends who'd gone before us,
unrecognizable now? The gangplank
rattled on the pier, swayed a bit
as we descended; tiled cupolas gleamed,
dock workers babbled some language
that was no language at all. Nothing
was how we'd imagined it. We were starting
not to know each other, and already
were becoming strangers to ourselves.

WE CAN'T SEE YOU

But the soul, once it is separated from the body,
cannot see what is in space …
– Diadochus of Photikē

Don't think because we can't see you
as you see one another,
that we can't see you as you are.

Because we have no eyes, we see
by love what love assimilates,

how your fucked up life
is adding up in time

without the graceful gestures and
accomplishments
of which you are so proud.

Icons show departing souls
as infants wrapped in swaddling clothes.

IN THE DREAM

You know the time has come;
you must wake up now.
                              – Rom. 13.11

You are riding on a bicycle's handlebars
but somehow flying over the Hawaiian islands
pointing out volcanoes to two men
you think are with the CIA. Then you enter
a bar full of dangerous criminals
which becomes a train reaching its terminus
and you get off, leaving your coat behind.
None of this makes much sense,
and there are other things which you realize
upon awakening can't be put into words.

In a courtyard a group has gathered around
the master's disciple, asking her questions
about the end of the world which is coming soon.
Someone asks about ninjas. That's just stupid,
you think, looking up to the grey clouds
for some sign of the apocalypse.

You know the time has come.
You must wake up now.

'Detachment from the dreams of the world',
you said to Fr. Worash. 'Yes', he said;
'that's what it means', he said. 'Eternity', he said.

METROPOLITAN

*At times Milwaukee has been just a little bit – shall we say, backward
– about doing things that lend society a metropolitan air. Polo games,
for instance, and riding to hounds.*

– Jeanette Juneau,
The Milwaukee Journal, 1924

Let us by all means take up the mallet;
let us ride to hounds in pursuit of the wily fox.

Breweries and tanneries humming with industrious
    workers
well-housed in snug cottages
enable us to engage the mind in higher things.

Meat-packing may be the means, but the end is
    sophistication:
the heads and tails of foxes lining the walls of our
    dens.

POLITICAL RESPONSIBILITIES

*Herod feared John, knowing that he was a righteous
and holy man, and he protected him. When he heard him
he was greatly perplexed, and yet he liked to listen to him.*

– Mk 6.20

King Herod was an educated man,
certainly no bigot, a Jew, but personally
open-minded, and interested in religion.

So, when the magi came with their story
about a star, he listened,
and commanded them to return
when they'd found this new-born 'King of the Jews'.

And he liked listening to John the Baptist,
though of course he had to have him arrested:
imposing one's personal morality on others
could only cause trouble, and his prophecies
of one who would 'baptize with fire'
were potentially destabilizing.

The Essenes, too, had some very interesting ideas
about the ascetic life in preparation
for the advent of a messiah,
but were attracting too many followers,
so their community had to be obliterated.

Sophisticated people could entertain these
intriguing ideas, but the uneducated were liable
to take them literally, causing problems
for men like himself with political responsibilities.

The Notification

came unexpectedly. I had thought
there'd be something in the papers
like before an election
or with daylight savings time,
but there was just the letter.
Report, it said – to some address
in the industrial valley where the stockyards
used to be. So it wouldn't be like the rapture,
a field full of folk awaiting the ascent.

I went, the next morning – they didn't give you
much notice, and how did they know
I had Tuesdays off? – at 9:30,
a bit early for me. The cattle
were gone but remnants of the abattoirs
remained. The door at the address given
opened onto a ramp – a joke, I thought,
and it must have been since I was the only one there,
but maybe others were coming later.

It was to be kind of like an interview,
is what I'd gathered. The old word,
'Doomsday', which they still used
had taken on misleading connotations;
it really just meant 'judgment',
which might turn out to be a good thing.

The ramp, or maybe it was just a corridor,
led to a room with a stained concrete floor.
I scanned the walls and ceiling for
claw marks, chains, fake showerheads.
Nothing.
Silence.

Then footsteps and a metal door I hadn't seen
opened and the judge came in
and I realized I was naked
which is usually a pretty good sign
you're dreaming, but in a dream no one notices,
and the judge, if that's what he was, said,
'You appear before me naked'.
'Yes', I said.
'So you're not dreaming', he said.
'No', I said.
'And do you know why you're here?' he said.
'For the interview', I said.
'No', he said, 'for the judgment'.

'I thought there'd be questions', I said,
'and I could explain things'.
'The evidence has been submitted', he said,
'the interrogation completed,
the sentence passed'.
I looked at the floor; there was nothing to say.

The door clanged; I looked up. He was gone.
An hour passed.
Silence.
Was I allowed to leave? I turned and went
the way I'd come, ready to hurry back
if I heard anything.
Nothing.
I went out, I was wearing clothes again,
and caught a bus home.

That was years ago. For the first year,
every day I expected a letter with the sentence,
but nothing came, so I guess it doesn't matter.
Nothing matters anymore.

The Making of Meaning

'In my poetry', says Joe,
'I allow space
for the reader to interact
with the text
in the making of meaning'.

That might work for Joe,
an easygoing guy,
but as for me, I want
my meaning fixed
like a nail in the reader's head.

THE CHEESE PLATE

Dublin, circa 1968, Br. Antoninus
at lunch in the Unicorn
enjoying the cheese plate,
of the Irish blue remarks,
'An interesting cheese;
not as sharp as the continentals';
later, of the cigar, 'A nice, fresh cigar',
before we drive him to St. Savior's Priory
to put on friar's robes,
and then to Synnot's Lounge
to read dramatically
a long poem on ecstatic fucking.

Not long after,
he abandons the Dominicans
and grows a beard so big
he names it 'William Everson'.

TO AN OLD PHILOSOPHER IN MILWAUKEE

A comfy condo on a leafy street beside
a gracious park, within a block a bank,
two wine shops and a cinema are all he needs
as life winds down to counting up accomplishments:
professor of philosophy, the book on Wittgenstein,
the volumes of well-crafted verse, a marriage,
a divorce, a few quite satisfactory affairs.

Though eros like a cinder unexpectedly sometimes
flares up with momentary heat,
he's glad those days are gone, fraught with desire.
Late sunlight streaming through a window
glows upon on a wall; it's lovely light, he thinks,
illuminating gently his remaining years,
waiting for nothing in particular to come.

JERUSALEM

And I saw the holy city, the new Jerusalem,
coming down out of heaven from God,
prepared as a bride adorned for her husband.

– Revelation 21.2

It was considered bad form to take notice,
a social blunder, but there it was:
a gigantic edifice of gold, transparent as glass,
descending, with its gates of pearl, river
bright as crystal, tree of life producing fruit
in every season, all aglow in perpetual light,
descending beside us, around us, within us.

We were nearly overwhelmed with love,
but did our best not to show it,
and were assisted in this by the institutions
we had built up in the old Jerusalem
while we were waiting for the new one
to arrive, never really expecting that it would,
and in the meantime having to live
in the old dispensation, a well-balanced
system: ambition, rivalry,
getting ahead at the expense of others
who were eager to get ahead at ours.

But there it was, an embarrassment
to everyone. After the initial confusion –
no one was quite sure anymore what was
acceptable behavior – we knew
things couldn't go on like this. In the end,
we convinced ourselves it wasn't there at all.

After my mother died and I had returned to the
campus ministry at Marquette, I saw that a speaker
was coming to give a lecture on grieving. I forget his
name. I thought, well, I'll go to that.

So I went to the talk. He said grief has a limit: you
grieve for four months, and then it's over. When he
said that, I got up and walked out. I'd passed my four
months, and I was still grieving, so he didn't have
anything to say to me.

Suffering and grief are good. Suffering is holy ground.
Grief shows how much love we had for the person
we've lost. As I said to my mother on her deathbed
after she'd died, 'So long, Ma. See you later'.

TOMORROW

In China it is already tomorrow
while here it is still today.

I watched on flightstats.com
your little yellow airplane
crossing the Rockies, the Sierra Nevada,
heading up the coast of California,
over Alaska and the Bering Straits,
inching across the satellite map's blue ocean.

I left the computer on that page all day
until the plane stopped in China and you got out
into tomorrow which for you is today
and where I am now is yesterday.

Et Cetera

Crying you entered the world;
leave it smiling.

*

Without sexual attraction
we might be polite,
but no one would fall in love.

*

Before Rimbaud, said Paul Valéry,
poetry had to make sense.

*

A rhymer and a poet are two things.
– Ben Jonson

*

… attention should always be given to some more
important points in which one has experienced
understanding, consolation, or desolation.
– Ignatius of Loyola

*

Speaking of a late beloved friend,
he used the present tense.

*

Who could ever invent the Blessed Virgin?
– St. Thérèse of Lisieux

*

A heart torn in two, flopping
like a fish on the riverbank.

*

The valley of tears leads
to the valley of tears.

*

Still expecting mother's phone calls.
Ten years.

*

Don't you think the only subject
for poetry is pain? said the poet
whose wife had left him,
taking out a restraining order.

*

He is the one man who kisses me
on the mouth and embraces me,
said Fr. Nelson in his homily,
speaking of his brother.

*

The little boy
reaching up for the chalice,
taking a big swig.

*

Alexander the coppersmith did me a great deal of
harm; the Lord will repay him according to his deeds.
– 2 Timothy 4.14

*

[Menedemus] shirked work, it is said, and was
indifferent to the fortunes of his school. At least no
order could be seen in his classes, and no circle of
benches; but each man would listen where he
happened to be, walking or sitting, Menedemus
himself behaving in the same way.
– Diogenes Laertius, II.131

*

There is a story that the boys laughed at
[Anaximander's] singing, and that, when he heard of
it, he rejoined, 'Then to please the boys I must improve
my singing'.
– Diogenes Laertius II.2

The man and the boy were in love
until the boy's parents found out,
took the boy to the police station,
and demanded he swear a complaint.

The boy resisted, but the parents
would not relent.
And so the man was arrested, convicted,
and sentenced to prison for a very long time,

and the boy, disturbed, assaulted
a younger boy, killing him,
and was arrested, convicted,
and sentenced to prison for a very long time,

so the laws of the nation were upheld,
and justice seen to be done.

Let's Talk

Cease doing evil. Learn to do good,
search for justice, rescue the oppressed,
be just to the orphan, plead for the widow.
Come, let us talk this over, says Yahweh.
– Isaiah 1.17–18

'Talk this over'? Is he kidding?
No, he's willing to hear the evidence
justifying injustice, favoring oppression,
the reasons for making life
harder for widows and orphans.

He figures there must be some pretty convincing
arguments supporting these positions,
since they are held by so many, and shape
the domestic and foreign policies of nations.

Let's hear them, he says; let's talk this over.

Though the account is common,
the many live, however, as though
they have a private understanding.

– Heraclitus, fr. 2

The individual, self-contained,
assured of himself, answering to no one,
judging everything by his own measure,
independent, unconstrained by tradition,
and the superstitions of the priests,
is an idiot, from the Greek 'Idiōtēs',
a man of private thoughts,
not fit for public office,
producer of worlds uninhabitable by others.

THE GODS OF REASON

The Gods of Reason take their seats
on the stage of the auditorium;
they are tall, male, calm and assured,
their luxurious locks streaked with gold.

They have come to refute the proposition
that gods exist, and will do so convincingly,
for they are the Gods of Reason.

'These so-called 'gods' before you',
say the Gods of Reason, gesturing
towards a few inferior gods invited
to present the case for the opposition,
'the gods of love, of peace, and of detachment,
are projections of the weak and lonely
longing for acceptance, embarrassed
to assert their will, ashamed
to embrace their desires; they objectify
their fantasies, and call them "gods"'.

'Wait! Wait!' the little gods protest,
'Let us speak for ourselves'.

But the audience is already jeering,
'There are no gods', they say, 'you don't exist',
and the little gods fade to neuroses,
which the Gods of Reason
push from the stage with a pointed syllogism.

Defeated, the shabby gods shuffle
into the street among the people
who recognize them as people recognize
celebrities, letting them know, shyly,
with a glance, that their presence

WARBLE

A proliferation of feelings
engaged them for a while
with the amazement that
other people felt things, too,
but feelings were untrustworthy
advertisements
for an unsubstantial self;

behind them lay
the mechanisms of perception
and the psychic structures
by which the world was made –
promising subjects
for scientific study,

but to what point
if language itself was nothing
more than lies
manufactured by
oppressive ideologies?

Liberated
from the hegemony of grammar,
words became multivalent
markers of ambiguous
possibilities – a shimmering
veil stretched over the abyss,
where on a shaky throne
sat meaning once.

If nothing could be said,
they still could warble, which
over and over again they did.

Works Cited

Augustine. *Confessions*. Trans. Henry Chadwick (Oxford, Oxford UP, 1991).

Chuang Tzu. *The Complete Works of Chuang Tzu*. Trans. Burton Watson (New York, Columbia UP, 1968), p. 49.

Conze, Edward, ed. *Buddhist Texts Through the Ages* (New York, Harper and Row, 1964).

Diadochus of Photikē. *Following the Footsteps of the Invisible: The Complete Works of Diadochos of Photikē*. Trans. Cliff Ermatinger (Collegeville, Minnesota, Liturgical Press, 2010).

Diogenes Laertius. *Lives of Eminent Philosophers*. Trans. R.D. Hicks (Cambridge, Harvard UP, 1970).

Heraclitus. *Fragments*. Trans. T.M. Robinson (Toronto, U of Toronto Press, 1987).

Homer, *The Iliad*. Trans. Robert Fagles (New York, Viking, 1990).

Ignatius of Loyola. *The Spiritual Exercises*. Trans. Louis J. Puhl, S.J. (Westminster, Maryland, The Newman Press, 1954).

Jonson, Ben. *Timber*. Ed. Ralph S. Walker (Syracuse, NY, Syracuse UP, 1953).

Plotinus. *The Enneads*. Trans. Stephen MacKenna (New York, Larson Publications, 1992).

Thérèse of Lisieux. *Her Last Conversations*. Trans. John Clarke (Washington, DC, ICS Publications, 1977).

Worash, Fr. James. Sermons preached at Church of the Gesu, Milwaukee, Wisconsin, 2011.

Jim Chapson, born in Honolulu, Hawaii, in 1944, was educated at San Francisco State University, and now teaches satire and other forms of writing at the University of Wisconsin-Milwaukee. He has had chapbooks published by White Rabbit, hit & run, and Blue Canary presses. His first book-length collection, *Daphnis & Ratboy*, was published by Arlen House in 2009, followed by *Scholia* in 2011.